Best Wishes
from Ethel Co

Blackberries and Crubeens

Tralee Childhood Memories

(in poems, prose and photographs)

Ethel Corduff

Rainbow Valley Books

First Published in 2023 by Rainbow Valley Books
Bula Matra House
205 Sanderstead Road
South Croydon
CR2 0PH

www.rainbowvalleybooks.com

Illustrations are from the public domain, or originals
Cover Design: Michael Round and Ethel Corduff
Main Text Set in Times New Roman 11.5
Published by Rainbow Valley Books
ISBN: 978-1-7392316-6-8
f

Printed and bound by CPI Group (UK) Ltd, Croydon, CR0 4YY

Contents

Editor's Note

This personal collection forms an eclectic memoir of an Irish girl growing up in the town of Tralee. Though slightly edited from the originals, the pieces were written at different times with a view to the compiling of a small anthology of memoir pieces. The poems appear for the first time in their present form. Some have been read at Croydon Writers' meetings and others workshopped through the Poetry Folio of the Society of Civil and Public Servants Writers. The photographs in some cases are over 70 years old, faded, and damaged, so some restoration has been necessary, but they still carry their visual narrative.

Author's Foreword

I should start with crubeens for those unfortunates who have not heard of them and thus missed something in life. Crubeens (from Irish crúibín, meaning 'pig's trotter') are an Irish dish made of boiled pigs' feet.

Blackberries were a huge part of my childhood, free and plentiful in surrounding fields, even earning pocket money

I love exploring the past and I wanted to capture my childhood in verse, later adding prose and photographs to enhance.

The studio and street photographers' photos are still clear and detailed. I am happy to share them. There are many more childhood incidents I could recount, perhaps for another time. I chose for this book those tales I remembered most from an often-carefree childhood.

Acknowledgements

I wish to thank the members of my Poetry Workshop Folio for the helpful critiques and comments of my childhood poems. Much appreciation to my editor, Michael Round. I am grateful for his expert advice, patience, expertise and high standards. The rose photographs were kindly provided by Vernon Hawkes who retains copyright.

Dedicated to my late parents
Maisie and Edward Walsh with thanks for a memorable childhood

Above: Upper Castle St Tralee. Postcard, about 1920, photographer unknown.
Below: Our two shops about 1960. My father is in window.

Introductory Photographs

Grandmother Catherine Kelly, Aunts Winifed (standing) and Hannah (sitting).

My Mother Maisie Kelly, her brother Denis,
Sisters Hannah (sitting) and Winifred.

Mother Maisie Walsh nee Kelly. Father Edward Walsh. On their wedding, 1939.

1
Celebrating My Beginnings

Even though I have always been interested in exploring the past and in recent years have researched my family tree, I had never really thought about where I was actually born. I was born in Tralee, County Kerry, Ireland. My short birth certificate, which was cheaper and adequate then, only gave place information with my date of birth. My mother's untimely death prevented me questioning her further.

About twenty years ago, I went to visit my cousin Eileen who was in hospital in Killarney and in the course of our conversation, she said, 'I remember the night you were born.'

I was astonished.

'Were you at the hospital, then?' I worked out Eileen must have been fifteen years old at the time.

'You were born at home. I was there with my mother, and your father drank tea out of a saucer.'

I was speechless at the thought of my frustrated-intellectual father who had travelled the world and often read *Time Magazine* from cover to cover and was the only person in County Kerry to read the *Manchester Guardian,* celebrating my arrival by drinking tea out of a saucer.

Her comments put all thought of further questioning about the day of my birth out of my head, to my regret.

Ethel Walsh about 1945, aged three.

2
Early Days

'**Give me more chocolate, Mammy,**' I cried, my small mouth already crammed with half a Cadbury bar, probably fruit and nut – that has always been my favourite. My tears had disappeared when Sister Baptista, petite and neat with thin-rimmed spectacles and black and white habit and veil, beckoned me into the classroom. I shrank from her and hid behind Mammy's bright coat. It was the very first time I had been so close to a nun. When I was four years old, you did not see any nuns just walking about the streets of Tralee, County Kerry.

The nuns kept to their Mercy and Presentation[1] Convents, schools, St Catherine's Hospital and Bon Secours Nursing Home. Even though the Presentation Nuns went to Mass at St John's Church, as we did, they only heard the Mass through the special windows of their chapel, which was parallel with the side of St John's altar. I used to be fascinated by this. Sometimes I would go up to the front pew to stare at them. They all looked like penguins from a distance, but when I got older, I could distinguish my teachers' faces.

I did not know it then, but Sister Baptista was absolutely wonderful with children, especially those terrified on their first day, like me. Pre-school playgroups were unheard of then, especially in Ireland. But in the infants' class at Presentation Convent School there were buckets and moulds to build castles, there were also plenty of building bricks

[1] The Presentation Sisters, officially the Sisters of the Presentation of the Blessed Virgin Mary, are a religious institute of Roman Catholic women founded in Cork, Ireland, by the Venerable Honora 'Nano' Nagle in 1775. The Presentation Sisters' mission is to help the poor and needy around the world. Historically, the Sisters focused their energies on creating and staffing schools that would educate young people, especially young ladies. Most of these schools are still in operation and can be found across the globe.

and piles of Mala (known universally as *Plasticine*). We had paper for drawing or crayoning and blunt scissors for cutting.

There was a lot of poverty in Southern Ireland. Children had few toys, so the classroom was like a treasure trove. I nearly forgot about Mammy[2] hovering in the background, loath to leave me, but happy I was enjoying myself.

Sister Baptista always stands out as a shining example of all a nun should be: kind, warm, humorous with a genuine interest in children and an outstanding teacher. The infants' class would now be called a reception class.

I still remember that group class photograph, a few days after I was admitted. This was a big event and Mothers came to watch and keep us tidy. That was the only official photo I ever had taken at school, and it was unusual for that time. Photos were a luxury then. Now schoolchildren have individual and group pictures from playgroup onwards.

I cried. I did not want to join in the photo but Mammy produced Rolos or Scots Clan to persuade me, I remember they were chocolate-covered caramel toffees. She gave some to the other children. Mammy was always doing things like that; she was a very giving person. That day the 'giving' was not a good idea as chocolate-stained faces needed wiping before the photograph. I was wearing a peculiar gym slip with a big ribbon in my hair. Most of the girls had hair ribbons. I still have that picture. Whenever I mull over it, I think of all the children in the photo and wonder what happened to them.

In the forties and fifties in Ireland, there was always a street photographer hanging about the town centres and particularly in Tralee, as few people had cameras then. He often snapped us as we walked down the town with Mammy. You could view the pictures in a lending library near Denny Street and buy one if you liked it and could afford to but there was no obligation to buy.

[2] I should mention that Mammy, even after marriage, was generally known as Maisie Kelly, her maiden name. This was not uncommon in Ireland.

I remember one photo which we called *Mammy coming out of jail,* taken outside Revington's in the Mall. It was Wednesday, early closing day, and the black wrought-iron gates were closed and looked very forbidding. Mammy was wearing a black and white check coat and a black hat at an angle. She loved clothes and was always bringing home clothes on approval, which meant you could go into any drapers in the town and bring home a few items for yourself or a member of your family to try on. If you liked one, you could buy it, even though in Mammy's case she often could not afford what we chose – but she would buy it, anyway.

Mammy liked *Ryle and Nolan* best. It was a small, very smart shop with joint owners Mrs Nolan and Mrs Ryle, whose husband was in charge of the local ESB (Electricity Supply Board) and whose daughter Una was in my class. They sold very high-quality clothes in their lovely double glass-fronted shop.

Back to the Presentation Convent School. As mentioned, Sister Baptista was a wonderful person and an excellent teacher. She became a good friend of Mammy, perhaps because Mammy was a very generous person, always giving things to the poor. I recall her giving parcels of used clothes in good condition for the poor children, of whom they were many then in Tralee.

Some years ago, on a nostalgic visit to Tralee, I visited Sister Baptista in the luxurious convent parlour. Though retired for several years, she kept her happy features, twinkling eyes, humour and love for humanity, especially children. I am sure many past pupils retained lifelong fond memories of her.

She told me that very day she had been to local solicitor Gerald Bailey's funeral. One of his daughters had been in my class right through school until secondary school. After that she went to boarding school, which was the custom of the local professionals' children. I remember Sister Madeline, in fifth class, favoured the children of professionals and had them sitting at the front in the class.

After finishing in 'babies' class' I moved, to senior infants in the building opposite, to the classroom of Sister Immaculata. She always seemed to have a red face with a temper to match. There seemed to be more crying in her class and not the same atmosphere. Some children who had been so settled with Sister Baptista, became unsettled. Some years ago, I met a classmate of my eldest brother Eddie who remembered my brother standing up for himself with Sister Immaculata.

I was glad to leave Sister Immaculata to go into first class with Sister Philomena, who was plump and homely.

Another early memory was buying meat at *Barrett the Butchers* at the corner of Moyderwell, the next street to where we lived. I was with Kathleen Callaghan who was in her teens; she was looking after me while my parents worked in our shop. We lived behind and above the shop,

Kathleen was tall with dark hair. I was about three years old and I did not like being told what to do. I did not want to hold her hand crossing the road, so I bit it, to my later regret. There were plenty of horses and carts coming and going to the creamery, and cyclists, but few cars. So she was only doing her job, even if I was in more danger from slipping in the dung from horses and cows. For biting, I got a good telling off and Kathleen was very upset.

I remember her Mother coming to talk to Mammy about the event as she was angry. Anyhow it was decided that Kathleen would not look after me anymore, maybe I was too naughty.

Not long after that, Kathleen went to work in England as so many did from Tralee and from all over Southern Ireland in the forties and fifties. Even though there were a few factories in the town, it was not enough for the young working population and wages were very low. Some shops paid only a pound a week in wages to start. It was almost expected that young people would go to England to work. Every year Kathleen would return for the Summer holidays. The first person she went to see, first time she came back, was 'Maisie', as Mammy was called. Mammy. called me out to the shop to see Kathleen and she laughingly recalled the day I bit her.

I also remember Mrs Callaghan, Kathleen's mother, very well. She was a large woman with snow white hair, always joking and laughing, and was one of our best customers. She usually wore a shawl. Years ago, about 95% of working-class Irish women wore shawls, big woollen brown ones with tassels at the edges, the shawl covered their heads as well. Some people would look down on women who wore shawls.

Some years ago I read *The Informer* by Sean O Callaghan[3], who was from Tralee, as I hoped it would invoke some memories of my home town. I thought there would be a connection to the Callaghan family we know to this day, as they were the only family of that name in the town with a population then of about 11,000, where a stranger would stand out like a gumboil. As I read, I found out that Sean was Mrs Callaghan's grandson. He described her as being very political and having no regard for authority. His family was Sinn Fein[4], and he followed his father and grandmother's politics. I was so surprised as I never knew of the family's political views and I could not visualise his grandmother as a radical.

[3] Sean O Callaghan, was a member of the IRA and turned informer. He died at the age of 63 in 2017. He apparently drowned in a swimming pool after a heart attack whilst on holiday in Jamaica visiting his daughter.

[4] Sinn Féin is an Irish republican and democratic socialist political party in both the Republic of Ireland and Northern island. The original Sinn Féin organisation was founded in 1905 by Arthur Griffith.

I never saw her or Kathleen march solemnly in the Easter Monday Parade wearing black berets and paper Easter lilies in their lapels along with the other local Sinn Féin families. In those days nothing happened with Sinn Fein it was mostly marches and meetings. Northern Ireland was a distant place, rarely mentioned and seldom visited by Southerners.

In some respects, I was lucky compared with other children as we had what people used to call a 'huckster's shop' which meant we sold a bit of everything: small groceries, fruit, vegetables, ice cream, cigarettes, periwinkles, dillisk[5], snuff, sweets such as toffee bars which were great value for a penny - Cough-no-mores[6] could give you a black tongue, Bull's Eyes, Aniseed Balls at twelve a penny. We sold the lot. I recall that when you sucked clear the aniseed, it left you with a tasteless ball in your mouth. 'Peggy's Legs' were a favourite: a short creamy rock, I tasted one last year, but it was totally different, much softer and cost a lot more than a penny.

My father was bald, and young yobs were continuously calling him names. When this boy whose father ran a local garage asked me for a pennyworth of 'baldy' sweets, I reacted immediately by lashing out at him; he left quickly without the sweets.

I remember friends from school and neighbour's children often called for me to play. Some would not play with me unless I brought them out sweets or buns. One friend ordered vanilla slices from me. Because I needed them to play with me, I would brave my father's wrath to pinch a Marshmallow Pig or a Geary's penny biscuit. My Mother might have given them to me, had I asked.

We had a shelf across the shop window in which we displayed the confectionery we ordered from *Havercroft's Bakery* across the road. Their cakes were delicious. We could always sell Chester Cakes[7], brown moist square cakes like bread pudding of today. Somebody saw

[5] Dillisk or Palmaria palmata is a deep red, or ferrous red, seaweed found in the pristine shores of the North Atlantic.

[6] Cough-no-more small liquorice toffee bar

[7] Sometimes known as Irish Gur Cake or Gur Slices.

them being prepared and said they were made with waste from other cakes and if you saw them being made, you would never eat them again. We also sold vanilla slices and sticky doughnuts in the evening as our shop was open from 7am until nearly midnight. Those slices were delicious washed down with Nash's red lemonade. It was a long day for my Mother as she was the one who was most in the shop.

Havercroft's also had a shop in the Square, their cakes were sought after, every morning usually Margaret Kelliher would come to take our order for the next day, We sold the buns mostly to country children from the local technical school or workers from the *Traly Footwear* and *Denny Bacon* factories, when they cycled home from work for lunch. They wore old clothes and no makeup but when they went out dancing or to the *Picturedrome* in the evening, they looked different – all made up and in matching clothes.

Geary's biscuits were very popular, they were delivered from Limerick They were large round dry biscuits currant or plain, we could not get enough of them as we only had a delivery every few weeks in the old square Geary's van, They were great value for a penny. If we could afford, we would have ordered more than two boxes at a time. But we lived week by week with no other income except from the shop and the small rent from the shop rented next door to *Halloran's Jewellers* and six of us to feed and clothe. There was little spare money.

The Infant School photograph. c 1946. Ethel seated front row wearing gymslip second from end.

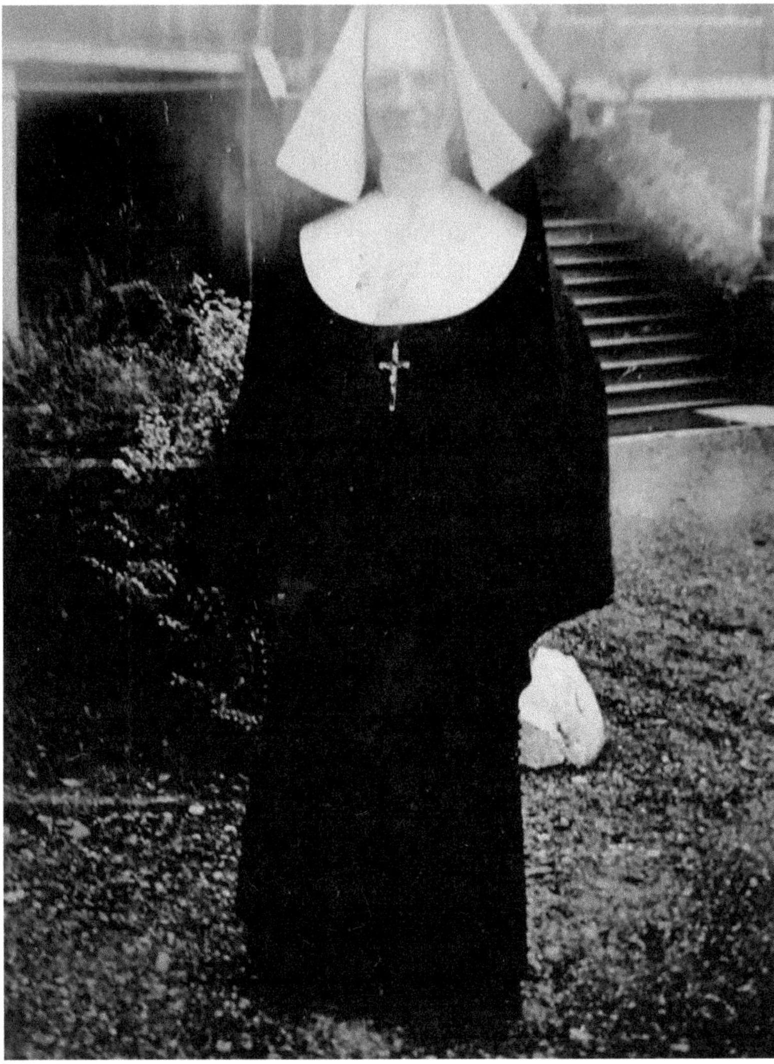

Sister Fintan O Hanion, born in Ashill. Ballymacelligot, Tralee. She was the oldest nun in Ireland when she died in 2005, aged 107. She was my mother's first cousin. She joined the Bon Secours nursing order in France, and nursed during two world wars and in Dublin and Cobh afterwards, before she died. The photograph was taken on a box camera in 1931.

3
A lasting impression

A human penguin gently
Took my hand from Mammy's,
Settling me between mala and sand
I was torn between the two delights.

I peeped at Mammy.
She smiled encouragingly.
I stuck a red plastic spade in the sand
And diligently filled a green bucket.

Sister Baptista waved at Mammy to go.
I got up to go after her
But she was too quick
Soon I was totally absorbed in play.

Sister Baptista was wonderful.
Gentle with the little ones.
I remember how happy
I was in that classroom then.

No one could match her love and attitude
After that auspicious year, school was a painful chore.
All the adult years I thought of her with affection.

In middle age, I returned to the convent to see her.
In her eighties, she looked slightly more lined
But little else not a wisp of hair was to be seen.
Sister Baptista welcomed me but barely remembered me.

She talked about how my mother helped the poor.
My sister, she recalled glowingly.
She told a cameo tale about my brother
The torch I had carried in my head extinguished a little.
Sometimes it is better to have only the memory.

4
More Memories

We had summer holidays in Ireland that lasted about three months. It was much too long and I remember days when I was very bored. Most families couldn't afford holidays unless they stayed with relatives. We were lucky in Tralee because we lived so near the sea.

At the other end of the town from where we lived was an area called The Basin which was like the beginning of a canal which was about a mile long leading to the sea at Blennerville. We often walked along the grassy path alongside the canal and ended up at the sea but there was no proper beach. To get to an actual beach was about six miles away and we could cycle there easily – mostly to Banna Strand, which was an almost deserted sandy beach with many sand dunes. Fenit was another destination, but the beach there was mostly pebbles, so we tried to spend time on the limited sandy section. Some Sundays, a train went to Fenit, which was always very full and popular. I only remember one small shop at Fenit and I think the Lock family ran it. We always bought something there. I loved the train as I suffered terribly from travel sickness even on a short bus journey and I remember once having to get off the bus in Pembroke Street as I was so nauseated.

We did not have any watches and I remember going to Derrymore Strand on the bus with my family. We were only there a short time when my mother saw the bus from Tralee to Dingle passing on the road. She said that we should go up to the road shortly to catch the bus when it came back, despite our protests that we needed more time, as we had not been on the beach for very long. She got some other families on the beach to come as well. Anyhow, it ended up being a quick day as we had only an hour on the beach so none of us were happy about it. She was always nervous about being late, but sometimes she overdid it.

Yet, we did have some holidays.

I remember we hired a cottage in Derrymore for a pound a week. It was very dilapidated, with few basic amenities, but it made a change and we were near the beach and our cousins the Buckleys were a short walk away. Hannah and Kathleen Buckley had been orphaned with their brothers at a young age and they were living in *Nazareth House Orphanage* in Tralee and they would spend the summer holiday with their aunt Maggie Buckley in Derrymore, so we saw them every day while they were there. When at home, we also visited them and also often took them on trips. I regretted we did not do the same for their brothers, who were in *Saint Joseph's Industrial School*, but my mother said she could not cope or afford to take more children on outings.

Another time, we shared a large house in Castlegregory with a family. I don't think it was a great success. We had a few brief holidays with my father's relatives in Waterford and Banagher, County Offaly, where my grandfather came from. I remember in Waterford I needed an adventure, so I planned to disappear for a while. I did not tell anyone. I got on a bus that went all around the city and stayed on it for a long time and my Mother was very relieved when I eventually returned.

Once, on our journey to Waterford by train, there was a delay in Mallow. I got off the train to buy something in the buffet shop and saw these strange packets I had not seen before. Enquiring what they were, I was told they were 'crisps'. I had never heard of them before and bought a packet. When I got back on the train, I dipped into it and my love affair with crisps started that day. I tried to get off the train to buy another packet, unfortunately, the train started moving. It was years before I saw crisps again.

I was a big reader. During the holidays I often read a book a day. Sometimes I had difficulty choosing a book from the local Carnegie Library, as I had read all the ones that appealed to me. I liked the Bobbsey Twin books and any books by Malcolm Saville and Noel Streatfeild who wrote *Ballet Shoes* and other shoe books and the *Chalet School* series by Elinor M. Brent-Dyer. I was not so keen on

Enid Blyton as I found some of her books repetitive, despite becoming a member of her Sunny Stories Club.

There were two lending libraries in Tralee for adults only. You paid to take out a book; I am not sure how it worked. The Healy family in Upper Castle Street had one and there was another near Denny Street which also displayed photographs that the street photographers took and you could order them there. There was no obligation to buy them as they took the photos without permission, but were more natural in that they were unposed. People often went to look at the display with no intention of buying any and I regularly did too.

I always looked forward to going back to school after the long summer holidays. Those long weeks away from school went back to the time children had to help with the harvest but we had no harvest in the towns. However, when I was into a week back at school, the excitement of the happy return from holidays fizzled out.

My favourite subjects were English and French. I recall great excitement when a 'Shakespearean speaker' came to visit the school occasionally. I also remember the class exchanging scrapbooks with a school class in another country. My struggles with algebra were completely negative and I should have been given help with trying to understand the subject as I always got nought in every test. It was frustrating in secondary school when, for the second year running, the same book, *A Christmas Carol,* was chosen, which I found so boring. We had to pay for all our school books.

There was a lot of poverty then which might have been a reason for not buying new books. In primary school, every morning, some children got free milk in a 'panny', a tin mug, and we often wished we could have the milk, too. Everyone went home for their dinner, which would be eaten at 1pm. There were no school meals then.

I was 'not very good with my hands', unlike my sister, who from her teens could make her own clothes. Needlework was definitely not my forte, and teachers criticised my work in our needlework class. One morning a school inspector was expected to visit and one item that would be looked at was knitted socks. I suddenly decided to take the day off and knit a pair of socks for the inspector. My mother agreed, and I spent the day in bed knitting. I worked all day and completed the socks and because I was so determined, the socks turned out fine. However, the next day, the teacher would not accept them as she did not believe I had knitted them as she had not seen me working on them. I could not win.

I enjoyed the cookery classes though, with Sister Petronella, even though my results were often not very edible. Sister suggested getting a bowl for my blood as I kept cutting myself. Queen of Puddings and Irish Stew were very popular in my young repertoire.

I also learnt the piano with Sister Kevin but I was not good at it and did not continue with her, though later on I learnt the piano from Dolly O Sullivan who lived in Boherbue. My main reason for being happy going to Dolly for lessons was because she had scrap books filled with news cuttings of the British Royal family. I was obsessed with finding out everything about them. So, I would go very early for my lesson, as it gave me an opportunity to look at them. Dolly organised concerts regularly for her pupils and neighbours in *Veal's Pub* outbuilding nearby and I took part in a few, playing a minor role as a gipsy in a sketch.

I had one very positive experience in sixth class with a wonderful teacher, Sister Mary John. She was much younger than the other nuns and I really enjoyed her lessons. One day we had to write a composition. I loved writing, and I wrote a story called *The Treasure Seekers.* She praised it and said I could become a writer. I was thrilled. After that, writing became more important to me.

When I was in secondary school, there was a small library, just one glass case of books each covered with brown paper. We covered all our books with brown paper as they were always passed on. Many of the books had religious themes with several by Annie Smithson.

Cora O Connor was a great friend in my class and also lived next to our school and a few doors away from me. Her parents had a shop too. It was a sweet shop called after her father Willie John. I remember once trying to hypnotise her. Also, I had heard soot was great for your skin, so we used it on our faces. I am not sure it did any good. At ten o'clock I never went home as directed and my father came to Willie John’s to tell me to go home.

After school, I often went with my friend Eileen Dore to her house in Casements Avenue where I was always made welcome by her Mother. I loved being in a house where the front door was closed unlike the open door in my house and I adored their garden. At that time I also became interested in photography as I had a Kodak Brownie camera and I sent away for a developing kit. Given permission to use their shed as a darkroom we started taking and developing photos. We even got orders for picture from school friends. A few of those photos are in this book.

We liked to visit our relatives who had farms around Tralee. Most of them lived within a four-mile radius in various directions and fairly remote areas. We had no transport and buses did not go anywhere near where they lived, but walking everywhere was the normal and usual thing to do then. We thought nothing of it. Regular visits were to our Grand Uncle, John Hanlon, and family, in Ballymacelligott. I remember, when he died, we were at the Wake and I was told to kiss him. It was the scariest thing to do, and I made sure I never did it again. When we were there, we played in the haggard (an enclosure beside a farmhouse in which crops are stored) and looked for the hens' eggs in the outbuildings.

There was another relation called Babe Sugrue who lived not far away from the Hanlons, and we often paid a quick visit there on the same day. We loved going to see Julie and Thady Tangney too, who were siblings and lived in Ballydunlea which was a long walk reached either from Ballyard or from Blennerville. Some of their land was rented out to the FCA (Local Defence Force) for shooting practice; we were never allowed near it as a result, but sometimes hearing the shots reminded us of the many cowboy films which were shown around that time.

Curragraigue was another favourite farm where the Griffin family lived. We called our elder cousin Aunt Elly, and I loved sitting with her and hearing her stories. She lived with her son, Paddy, and his family. Sadly, Paddy’s wife died very young, leaving two young children and a baby who was brought up by another of Aunt Elly's sons, Michael, and his wife. Every Sunday night Aunt Elly was at Michael's house in Moyderwell. I would 'granny sit' Aunt Elly there when Michael and wife Nell went to the cinema. We would have a freshly cooked apple pie to enjoy with our tea while we chatted away. I never wanted those evenings to end. We were also related to the Griffin family that lived in Cahills Park and I visited them too as I was friendly with their daughter Marie.

Because of our closeness to our farming relatives, when I was older, I was often asked to help them prepare for the 'Stations'. The Stations was a longstanding custom in the country. It came from 'The Stations of the Cross' and in Ireland was celebrated in a collective prayer and meditation event, with a feast afterwards. In our case, every year in each area, a priest would say a Mass in a house and the household invited all the neighbours. Each house was on a rota to host the event. However, the gathering involved massive preparations, as the entire house was decorated inside and out. The host family entertained the priest after the Mass in the best room with a special breakfast and only special people were invited to sit with him. I had the dubious honour occasionally of being one of the special folk.

We had other Hanlon relations in Ashill where my grandmother Catherine Kelly, née Hanlon was brought up. We did not visit often as we saw them on a regular basis as they supplied us with vegetables.

There was an incident once concerning a relative in our extended family. In our house we had a small bedroom which had a skylight. My mother heard a noise from the bedroom and went to investigate and found the young man climbing through the skylight, She got an awful fright. Apparently, he and some friends had been drinking in Madgie Reidy's illegal shebeen which was at the back of her shop a few doors away and it had been raided by the Garda and the relative and friends had escaped through the back. He had climbed over walls to reach our garden and got on a flat roof to reach the skylight.

Madgie Reidy's shop was a mess. Everything thrown together in the window. Some people said there were mice running around. It was surprising she did any business at all.

While I waited for something exciting to happen, with my friend Norah Ashe, we thought we could make some money. So, we started making bath salts with washing soda and perfume. However, this activity was put aside when we noticed a very well-dressed couple with two children shopping at Madgie's regularly. It mystified us as even the locals did not shop there.

Suspecting something strange and longing for excitement the next time they looked like going to shop there we followed them in and the lady was buying a bottle of whiskey on tick. We had to justify being in the shop so we bought some Cough-no-mores. My tongue was stained black for weeks afterwards, as they were probably out of date. We were so curious about this strange family in the town as they stood out at that time when people were leaving town rather than moving in. Eventually found out where they lived by following them, which was in 'The Kerries', a district in Tralee. We went there and knocked on the door and asked for a glass of water, saying one of us was not well. We were hoping they would ask us in, but that did not happen and we were handed a glass of water by one of the children. Anyhow, the mystery was solved when we found out they were from England, and the man was the new manager of the plastic factory. I discovered years later that he had embezzled the company of sizeable sums of money and there was a court case, so our suspicions that they were ne'er-do-wells were justified after all.

When the May Procession time began, I wanted to make an altar in our upstairs bedroom window ignoring the fact that few people would see it. We had a statue of Our Lady but needed roses to surround it. But where would I get roses? We only had a concrete back yard with not even a weed never mind a rose. Then I remembered, when we were in Foley's Forest during our backyard bazaar, seeing some wild rose bushes at Madgie Reidy's and at her sister Birdy's completely overgrown garden. After searching for some coins, I headed out to Madgie's. It surprised her that somebody wanted the wild roses and would pay for them. 'You can have them for two shillings,' she said. I had enough money and handed it over.

I had to pass through the illegal shebeen watched by a very surprised Birdy to get to the garden. All I recall now is how dark and dingy everything looked. I had to struggle through nettles and knee-high weeds to get to the thorny rose bushes. After gathering an armful of roses my arms and legs were scratched and sore. When I got home proudly carrying them, my father asked where I had got them.

'I bought them from Madgie Reidy,' I said proudly.

It was a mistake to say I had *paid* for them as he got so angry and tried to grab them from me but I ran off dropping some in my flight.

'She should never have charged you for those weeds I am going round to get the money back!' he yelled even as he headed out the door. I felt so embarrassed that he did that, but he instantly stood up for us very directly, in a way my mother would never do. She would take into consideration how we would feel, discussing the problem with us, before carrying out any action.

We used to play in Moyderwell which was just around the corner from Upper Castle Street which was too busy. One day when I was skipping with my friends, unknown to me, I was being watched by a young neighbour from their front room window and while doing so she accidentality broke a piece of china. It might have been a vase. Anyhow, her mother came out and blamed me for the accident. When I ran home upset and told my father he headed immediately to put her straight.

Some years later. when I worked in *Hurleys Book and Toy Shop* for two years from the age of fifteen and had not had a holiday and was complaining at home about it but was afraid to mention it to the owners as I did not know how to broach the subject or how they would react. One day Mrs Scanlon called me in to the office and said, 'I have had a letter from your mother complaining that you have not had a holiday all the time you have been here.'

I was upset and astonished that my mother would write a letter like that without discussing it with me. It was so unlike her to do that. However, I ended up with a week's holiday the following week. When I got home, I confronted my mother about the letter, she was astonished and insisted she did not write the letter, indeed would *never* have written it. My father who was listening admitted that *he* wrote it and signed my mother's name to it. We were both so angry with him. He may have smiled sheepishly but he did not apologise, just said, 'Thanks to me you have got your holiday.' So yet again he really stand up for family members though sometimes went the wrong way about it.

Even as a child, I understood my father's frustration with small-town Irish life in the forties and fifties as I sometimes felt its narrowness too. When he was in his sixties he would often spend six months in London sending a postal order regularly. He wanted us all to move to England but my mother was not interested; He ordered a Sunderland newspaper and gave it to me to read. The advertisements for shops and entertainment fascinated me. One day, a couple came to our shop and said they were interested in buying the place. Apparently, my father had advertised our shop without telling my mother, which she was not happy about. Mammy would never leave her beloved shop much to my father's dismay

Religion ruled our lives because we did not know any different. As an avid reader I lapped up the stories about going on exciting holidays, about boarding schools and midnight feasts, about guides, children's clubs and birthday parties and I longed for some of these exciting events being in my life. Even though we had freedom and friends and were surrounded by lovely countryside, I often felt unfulfilled and longed for more interesting activities. We had the free tickets to the cinema and Irish dancing and that was it. I was never at a children's birthday party because nobody had them then. On our birthdays my mother would get a Fuller's cake from *McCanns* and we would have jelly and custard, I only remember one occasion when my younger brother's godparents called on his birthday.

I remember the very exciting event of a Christmas bazaar in the Protestant Hall in Ashe Street where we had a fantastic afternoon tea and interesting stalls. By contrast at the CYMS (Catholic Young Men's Society) Christmas bazaar which lasted nearly a week there was little to buy except bundles of used magazines and I don't recall any food but the big attraction was the hamper raffle every night conducted by Maurice Curtin. My mother was very lucky and nearly won, or came close to winning, a hamper every night until it became embarrassing that she was winning so much.

One thing that still puzzles me to this day is that my mother took on the responsibility of collecting property payments, which I think were for ground rent, from several neighbouring shops on behalf of the Denny Estate who were absent landowners based in England. She then delivered the payments to William Giles Auctioneers in Denny Street. She did not like collecting it and as soon as I got old enough, she used to ask me to do it. The shopkeepers were never happy to see me coming, particularly Miss Curtin in Moyderwell. I do not know why Mammy had to do it or if she got paid. Once more I wish I had questioned her more about family happenings and history, about so many other things.

When I was fifteen and on the cusp of leaving school, I took on a holiday job *with Kennelly's Photographers* in Ashe Street It was not very busy so I was glad when it was First Communion Day and children came to have their photo taken. My Mother brought my brother Victor for his communion picture because I would be there, whereas we had always previously used *Healy's Photographers*, as they were in business for many years. I helped arrange Victor for his Communion Picture, which is in this book.

I remember one day Padraig Kennelly was getting ready to go to a wedding; he told me to get in the car. I got excited as I had never been to a wedding and to go as the photographer's assistant seemed so important. He drove up Ashe Street and parked outside his house and told me to get out and wait at the steps to his house while he went inside. After a few minutes, he came out and handed me some towels. 'These are for washing,' he said, and drove off to the wedding. After a week I told him I wanted to leave and his answer was: 'You are too thin.'

I wish someone would say that to me now.

5
A Tralee Childhood

Bring me out a Chester cake
and a Cough-no-more
and I'll play with you today
my friend would say.

Standing at the shop window,
scrutinised by my father, who
never wanted us to take anything.
Suddenly he was distracted by a customer
who wanted one Woodbine[8] and a match.

I grabbed a Chester cake and Money Ball[9]
and stuffed them up my sleeve
ignoring his cries
and ran out of the shop
to join my playmate.

We headed to Green Lane and called
for Derry and Tom Healy
I loved lifting up curly topped toddler Derry.
Years later, I found he had become a priest.

Often we played picky[10] on the pavement
by Petey Kelliher's garage or we headed down The Green.
I liked to borrow a baby in a pram to bring along
while we played on the see saw, swings or merry-go-round.

---

[8] Woodbine was the cheapest brand of cigarette.
[9] Money Ball: a round red sticky ball, very sweet, could contain a small coin if lucky.
[10] Picky is hopscotch.

Often after Mammy would pick us up after school
we would join her friends and children
Masons, Switzers and Flahertys in the town park.
Mammy doled out sweets, while we all played together.

Looking back, no tv, no phone, no car,
comics when read were sold for
half price by my father, daily outdoor play.
A book a day from the Carnegie Library[11]
and free cinema tickets for displaying posters
All the electronic gadgets and tablets could not compete.

Town Park bench Switzer brothers, Margaret Mason, Eddie, Ethel, Glória, Bernard and Vourneen Flaherty 1950s.

[11] Carnegie Library: free library

6
This House

The house where I was born
was not really the norm,
our door was always open
from morning until we lay down.

How I envied my friends
who could close their doors,
be at peace or war without
outsiders lurking or interfering.

Most had front gardens
ours had none
but a worn grey pavement
trod on by everyone.

We woke early morning
to cattle, mooing to market.
Once, an enormous cow dashed in,
got stuck outside the counter,
it was a horrendous encounter

We sat in a poky room,
facing a narrow netted window,
through which we saw customers
peering while awaiting serving.

Furnishings were sparse
our only income from the shop.
No carpets then, worn linoleum
and concrete floors were the norm.

To stop us reading in bed,
our father took out the light bulbs,
We read by torch instead.

Yet our friends envied us
as we lived in a sweetshop
which helped our teeth to rot

7
First Confession

We filed past the massive marble angels and up the aisle until we reached the Hansel and Gretal wooden house

If only it was play time not the dreaded event of purging our souls.

Sister indicated where we were to sit and made us join our hands in prayer. We heard the mutter of voices which the thick curtain could not hide.

Each time the door opened and a class mate bounced or skulked out, smirkng, smiling or scowling, nausea gathered higher in my throat.

'You're next,' Sister Philomena called. She grabbed my arm as I froze and pushed me in the dark alcove.

The head behind the grill nodded as I knelt slowly hoping the vomit would not spray him.

'Yes, my child?' He waited while I moistened my lips and tried to ignore the nausea.

'Bless me Father, I told a lie Father. It was only a little one Father. I said, "Caw Caw!", I pulled my brother's hair and he bawled.'

The priest covered his face. Were my sins so bad? Then he faced me. 'Now say an act of contrition before I absolve you from your sins.'

The words that had been drummed into us would not come. I trembled.

8
First Communion Memories

Looking back to my First Communion in Tralee in 1949, the main preparation was for confession, and the hardest thing was fasting from midnight. For that reason, the Holy Communion Mass was about 9am. My Mother came to the church. There were no guests, and I felt extremely holy. We knelt at the altar to receive the communion. That is my dominant memory of the church. Afterwards, I had a lovely soft-boiled egg and thick toast for breakfast.

I stood at our shop's front door in my finery, swinging my white handbag, hoping for some cash from our customers and passer-bys. Admiration and congratulations, made up partly for the lack of cash, as there was very little forthcoming. But more importantly, my father gave me sixpence. It was the first money he had ever given me. He was very tight with cash. It felt as good as if he had given me a pound, for sixpence was a sizeable sum to a child then.

I had a studio photo taken in *Healy's Photographic Studio* beside a basket of lilies; I presume they considered the lilies a sign of purity. Later, my mother took me and my siblings to the Lee Strand Dairy for their delicious freshly made ice cream covered in strawberry sauce in glass dishes. It was the *ultimate* treat then.

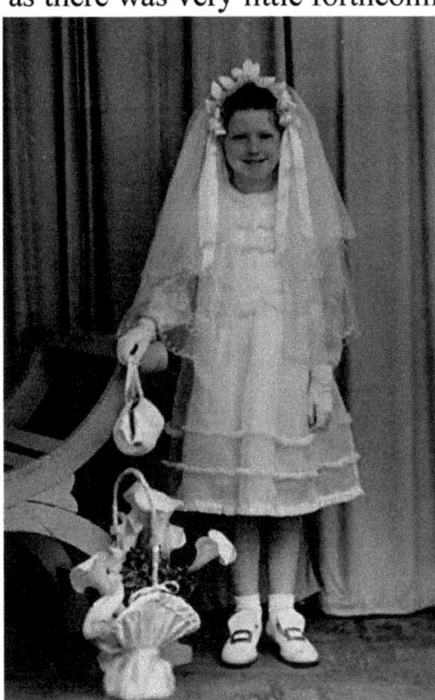

Ethel's First Communion 1949

9
Through the Shop Door

I lived where all life
passed through the door,
open all hours like
Ronnie Barker's shop.

The door was sky blue
painted so in later years
with a large heavy key and sturdy lock,
when it was bolted, I felt secure.

It was closed from midnight to 6 am,
not needing an alarm
Mammy clambered out of bed
while my father slept on.

First through the door
cycles left standing on kerb
were the workers
heading for Denny's Bacon
and Traly Footwear factories.

Next might come a relative
bringing vegetables freshly dug
from their farm in Ballymac.
Mammy would arrange the cabbage and
parsnips
on the stool outside, where they were
prodded by every housewife passing by.

Then the school kids
looking for Cough-no-mores, Peggy's Legs,
twelve a penny Aniseed Balls
or a pink Marshmallow Mouse
which disappeared too quickly.

Mammy behind her beloved counter.
Queen of all the products she carefully displayed.

10
Service from a young age

Our little shop was at the poor end of the main street, ironically called Upper Castle Street. The important end with the banks and big shops was called Lower Castle Street. Our shop was a type of huckster shop selling anything and everything as mentioned earlier. We made every penny count: dillisk seaweed was gathered and dried on the seashore, often by us; the periwinkles we sold we also gathered and cooked in our kitchen in a big pot with a whole packet of salt. We usually bought vegetables from relatives who had farms outside the town. The farmers' wives often brought eggs to us to exchange for tea and sugar on Sunday mornings after Mass.

Bread was the most important food in the fifties, especially as it was scarce during and after the war years. I remember when I was about three and a half, hidden behind the counter while Mammy served customers. A woman asked for a loaf of bread, of course, I did not realise my Mother kept the limited stock of bread for regular customers. When Mammy said we did not have any, I piped up, 'Oh, yes we have.' That must have been very embarrassing for Mammy.

My father did not like shop keeping. After all, he had worked on a ship and had even tried to get work as an actor in Hollywood – but he did like to introduce new ideas. I must have been about eight when *Thompson's*, a big baker in Cork city over sixty miles away started making sliced bread. It created a huge interest. My father heard about this and contacted *Thompson*'s by phone. I am not sure how he did that because making phone calls was rare then, and only the bigger shops had phones.

Anyhow, soon we were one of the first shops in our town to have sliced bread delivered from Cork. I was excited on Tuesdays and Thursdays because the big *Thompson's* van pulled up outside and the driver lugged the bread into the shop in an enormous wicker basket. People were queuing up to buy it. We had to ration it to one loaf per person. We also sold confectionary for *Havercroft's Bakery* just across the road.

We had a shelf going along the length of the front shop window laden with trays of buns. The favourites were vanilla slices. We did well because *Havercroft's* was closed in the evening and on Sundays when we were open and busy.

At lunchtime, the children who went to the local technical school bought buns and ate them with red lemonade to wash them down. The factory girls from *Denny's Bacon Factory* and from the *Traly Footwear* factory got off their bikes to take the buns home to have with their dinner. In a small town like Tralee, everyone walked or cycled home for dinner at one o'clock.

I lived only ten doors away from the *Presentation Convent* where I went to school. Mammy always had dinner ready for one o'clock despite running the shop. Father ate his dinner first at twelve o'clock. Then he was often out inspecting any new building being built. He was particularly interested in those with flat roofs, as there were very few of them in Tralee. I often served customers in my lunch break and helped myself to some sweets as a reward. On the counter top we had a glass display case. The top was partly worn from the passing of coins. You had to peer in to select from the penny sweets, Cough-no-mores, Money Balls, Marshmallow Mice, Peggy's Legs and Aniseed Balls.

No wonder I used to suffer from severe toothache. I would go into the chemist next door and Mr. Irwin would dip some cotton wool in a tooth tincture and put it in one of the painful cavities.

Other children because of the sweets blackmailed me; they often would not play with me unless I brought out sweets to them. They would give me an order for a particular favourite. I risked my father's wrath if he caught me, which was frequent, as it was difficult to hide a vanilla slice or doughnut up your sleeve.

Poverty and austerity were rife in Ireland in the 1940s and 1950s; sweets were often a rare luxury especially as most people had big families. We were envied because we had access to them 'without paying'. My Mother was very easy going and would not stop us taking them to give away; she had great sympathy with the poor children. Being the eldest, I was of course number one for helping in the shop. We were often very busy, especially on Sunday nights when many married and courting couples went to the pictures.

We were only a few doors up the street from the *Picturedrome* and everyone brought a 'quarter of sweets' to suck during the programme. When we were young, Mammy would buy us comics for Sunday evening to keep us quiet as both she and Daddy had to serve, as there were so many sweets to be weighed.

We sat in the room behind the shop reading the *Beano*, the *Dandy* and *Schoolfriend.* Mammy could see us through the window in the room and we could see her. When we had read the comics, my father folded them tidily and put them inside the scratched display case and sold them for half price.

My brother Eddie nearly two years younger than me, hated serving in the shop and if he was going out and saw customers standing there, he would shout, 'Shop!' and rush out into the street. I used to get very angry about this. It was ironic that years later that he would have a shop of his own.

11
Cloghers Orchard

We had long Summer school holidays in Ireland
Originally because of helping with the harvest
But in the town there was no hay to be collected
And going on holidays was a rare event.

Mammy ensured we were kept busy
But she tried to make it fun.
She left my father to mind the shop
When we took the long trek up Ballymullen.

Victor in his pushchair, Eddie and Gloria
and I lagging in the heat until we
reached Cloghers House, the original home of
William Mulchinock, who wrote the Rose of Tralee.
Inspired by Mary, the kitchen maid.

We headed for the orchard behind the house
Where Mammy discussed what was ripe
with Mr Naughton the gardener.
While we tucked into strawberries.

He directed to the best apples and pears
Sometimes we would pick ripe gooseberries
We started filling buckets, when they were full
We stopped for Nash's red lemonade and Havercroft's buns

Mr Barron the owner would deliver the fruit in butter boxes
On his way to work as Manager of Denny's Bacon Factory
Mammy would haggle as she wanted to sell them cheap.
Fruit was a luxury to most families then.

12
Family Fortunes
The Raffle

In Lower Castle Street there was a large newsagent, book, school stationers and toy shop – *Collins*. In the fifties toys were in short supply. With little money to spend they were mostly sold at Christmas. *Collins* would open a display upstairs and toys could be put away and paid for in instalments.

We visited *Collins* regularly for our comics and on one visit in the summer we were told, probably by our cousin Eileen Horgan who worked there, that there was going to be a big raffle with two prizes – a tricycle and a toy motor car with pedals. This was unheard of and a source of great excitement among the children in the town. We immediately got our mother to buy some tickets, and we started counting the days, continually visiting to look at the magnificent prizes. I coveted the tricycle.

Finally, after several weeks, the day arrived when the prizes were going to be drawn on a Wednesday afternoon as it was half day closing. The shop was packed with children clutching tickets I was there with my sister Gloria and brother Eddie. My younger brother Victor was still an infant.

It took ages for the tickets to be all folded and put in a big box by Bridie Nolan the manager. At last the prizes were drawn the first ticket pulled out was the second prize which was the motor car and the ticket pulled out was the one belonging to my brother Eddie. I had not wanted the car so was pleased for him. When that excitement died down attention turned to the draw for the the tricycle prize and 'Gloria Walsh' was called. There was discord all around us and people were muttering 'Fiddle 'Fiddle'. I wasn't happy either and started crying, Bridie gave me a painting book to pacify me but it did not appease me at all.

When we got home, I went under the stairs and cried my heart out while my brother and sister headed straight out to the backyard with their prizes. I was startled by loud cries and looking out, my brother was trying to pull my sister off the bike. Apparently, he had difficulty reaching the car pedals as his legs were too long. Despite my tears I was secretly pleased.

Ethel in Irish dancing costume, sister Glória on raffle prize tricycle.

13
Chilly memories

Clutching my red hot water bottle
I climbed into bed in my fluffy socks
The sheets felt damp and cold
Winter in Kerry was always harsh.

I blamed Sliabh Mish for the constant rain
The mountain loomed over the town
And was a backdrop to Tralee Bay
where famine ships once departed.

Indoors the only room that
Was heated was a haven of cosiness,
I developed chilblains from hugging the coal fire,
Mammy once threw a ten-shilling note in
The flames, thinking it was a sweet paper.

We lived surrounded by concrete
Town outskirts were lush in comparison
When winter started subsiding, it was great to
See the spring flowers down the Green.

One day, my friend Norah and I were admiring
The Rose Garden, in honour of the Rose of Tralee.
Norah gently plucked a pink rose, raised it to her nose,
A shout rang out, she dropped it in a carpet of petals
Mr. Wynne the Park Gardener came running

14
Dillisk and Periwinkles

Mrs Doran and Castlegregory Fishermen
Supplied our shop with sea produce,
Dillisk and periwinkles
If low supply, we headed for the shore.

We scrambled among rocks in Fenit
Slipped on seaweed in Derrymore
Searched in crevices and pools
For the elusive winkles.

Dillisk picked off the rocks
we spread on the beach
To dry in the sea breeze,
Doing so in our backyard
Loses its special salty taste.

When our basket was half full
Of live moving shells,
We turned the dillisk
Praying for no rain.

Mammy boiled the periwinkles
Adding salt to the pot.
We sold them by the panny
With a pin to pull out the slimy contents.

Dillisk was sold in small bags.
Emigrants returning home
Made their first shopping trip
To Maisie Kelly's
For their Kerry sea fix.

Brother Victor and Jill Mason holding dillisk, after beachcombing.

15
Confirmation

Looking back, my memories of Confirmation day are not like my memories of my First Communion Day which are very vivid. Confirmation was usually made when you were about twelve years old. Preparation was carried out in the school, unlike now when it is carried out in the parish and children have a choice whether to be confirmed or not. We had no choice. Presentation nuns mostly taught us in preparation. We would have catechism classes every day usually about midday. The Angelus[12] was said at midday when the church bells would ring and we would stop whatever we were doing to pray.

There would have been extra religious classes for Confirmation. I remember one class in particular, not sure if it was before Confirmation. We had to stand. I smelt burning and sizzling, and a girl called Carmel Lawlor who had a long plait was standing in front of an altar to Our Lady which had a lighted night light and her plait caught fire. Luckily, it was quickly distinguished.

Getting a new outfit for the Confirmation ceremony was essential and Mammy would only buy the best for such an important occasion nearly putting her into debt. I am wearing winter clothes so it was not summer, unlike First Communion, which was usually in May. The Bishop of Kerry confirmed us. He anointed each person with the oil of chrism[13] while saying, 'Be sealed with the Holy Spirit.' Then the confirmand said, 'Amen.' The bishop then shook the confirmand's

[12] The Angelus (Latin for 'angel') is a Catholic devotion commemorating the Incarnation of Christ. The name Angelus is derived from the first few words of the text: *Angelus Domini nuntiavit Mariæ* (The Angel of the Lord declared unto Mary).

[13] The third oil, holy chrism oil, is olive oil mixed with balsam. The oil symbolizes strength, and the fragrant balsam represents the 'aroma of Christ' (2 Cor 2:15). Anointing with chrism oil signifies the gift of the Holy Spirit. It is used to consecrate someone or something to God's service.

hand, saying, 'Peace be with you.' The reply, 'Also with you.' And that was it.

Confirmation was low key compared to First Communion. I don't recall anyone giving me money or having a special treat on that occasion.

16
I Remember

Biting my carer Kathleen Callaghan's hand
as I did not want to cross the road with her
to Barrett's Butchers in Moyderwell.
The toothache from nibbling at sweets in our shop.
Mr Irwin, the chemist next door dipping
cotton wool in a clove liquid to ease the pain.
Being offered nettle sandwiches at our cousins' and
disposing of them in the garden where they belonged.

Waking to the clatter of horses and carts going to the creamery.
My daily trip to the Carnegie Library looking for
Malcolm Saville, Chalet School and Bobbsey Twin books.
Scoffing apples, gooseberries and plums in Cloghers House
orchard
where the Rose of Tralee was a servant long ago.

The street photographer lurking down town to catch us unawares.
Catching my fingers on the clothes wringer never to be used
again.
Rash on my legs from sitting so close to the coal fire.
And Mammy with love.

17
Surrounded by Water

I grew up in a town
called Tralee
'Strand on the Lee'
Surrounded by water
in Tralee Bay.

We cycled to Derrymore
the sea on our right
Banna Beach was a different route
where we hid in sand dunes
Roger Casement was arrested here
in 1916 for treason.

Few could swim in the fifties
but my father had worked on ships
he taught us in freezing water
Gloria was a strong swimmer
Eddie became a lifeguard
But I kept my feet firmly on the sea bed
and never got out of my depth.

My poor Mother
Tormented by an underlying brain haemorrhage
at 5am walked the canal path
to Blennerville in Tralee bay
Seeking some relief.

18
Duffy's Circus is coming to town

At last we saw the huge trucks trundle
through the narrow streets,
we headed for the Fair Field.

We wandered among the caravans
gaped as the big top being raised,
stared at the muscular circus workers.
But which were the clowns?

A little man waddled past, dragging a rope
We were sure he was one and followed him.
suddenly he turned whipping the rope.
We fled screaming.

We could hardly sleep for excitement.
After school, we saw the tent was up
soaring majestically skywards.
Tomorrow, the clowning would begin.

The great day here at last
We queued on sawdust for the cheap seats
The band started playing as the ringmaster entered the ring
We joined in the roar of the packed tent.

'Bring on the clowns!'
The band reached a crescendo.
Into the ring cycled a tall clown on a penny farthing
wearing multi coloured clothes and a top hat
followed by two plump clowns boxing and frolicking.

We yelled and laughed
at their antics and tricks
No sign of the cranky little man.

19
Backyard Bazaar

I travelled Tralee town clutching leaflets
delivered where children lived.
Come in fancy dress to Walsh's Bazaar
17 Upper Castle Street
2pm Saturday.

The queue from 1pm stretched down the street.
My Father unwillingly kept control
while indulgent, Mammy welcomed them all
as I donned my Wee Willie Winkle nightgown.

The kids surged through the shop and house
eager for excitement during the long Summer.
Some were in homemade fancy dress.
My siblings manned the stalls.

The lucky dip full of old shoes wrapped singly
in newspaper, another dip to get a matching shoe.
Aniseed balls and Coughs-no-mores
secretly sourced from the shop were snapped up
diluted red lemonade soon sold out.

Old toys and well read Beanos and Dandys
were scrutinised some given away,
as cash was short
Trips to Foleys Forest over the wall
to our neighbour's abandoned orchard
popular for getting bruised apples

I put on my Madam Zena disguise for
fortune telling in the shed while
kids kept opening the door to eavesdrop.

The Talent contest rounded off the day
on a makeshift platform,
we listened to songs and jokes
Michael Donovan's great singing
was a clear winner.

Mammy was at hand as the kids left
doling out sweets to the empty handed
while my father buried his head in Time Magazine.

Dad in his favourite chair, probably the *Irish Times* on his lap.

20
Journey to Derrymore

Armed with swimming togs, buckets, spades,
Cheese and tomato sandwiches, red lemonade
We head to Tralee bus station.

We arrive early, argue over seats
I grab a window one as I need air.
During the three-month summer holiday
Derrymore was a favourite destination.

The green bus drove slowly down Ashe Street
into the Mall, lined with horses and carts
and a few dusty Morris Minors,
left onto narrow Bridge Street,
past the Dominican Church
with Sliabh Mish looming ahead.

Queen Scotia is said to have lived there
at its foot seagulls scoop, screech and scrape
for titbits at the town dump
What would the Queen think of that?

We look out for Blennerville Windmill,
hold our stomachs and yell as the bus roughly
manoeuvres the narrow hilly bridge.

There's the little people's shop'
yelled my little brother Victor.
Where they stand on raised planks
to reach the counter and customers.
. We pass Judge Johnson's gated house
secure from those sentenced *who* might take revenge.
Privacy is paramount now.

Through Tonevane and Curaheen, past Allman's shop.
In our teens we would drop our bikes and
pop in for a Lucan Dairy ripple ice cream while
Tralee Bay's still water glistens to our right.

Here's Maggie Buckley's, the bus slowed at the bend
we crane to see the hut behind the house
where our cousin lived when she had TB.
Nearly there now, we gather our belongings.

The bus creaks to a halt at the narrow lane leading
to Derrymore strand which we frequently
had to ourselves with seaweed, sand, shells,
the freezing water and nowhere to even spend a penny.

21
Promises

Some promises are hard to keep
In the confessional begging forgiveness,
then promising not to offend again.
Next week crawling back with the same sin.

Promises made at marriage
To honour, love and obey.....
Couples now choose their own words
agree their chosen terms.

A promise can be sacred
especially when it is a secret
not to be betrayed.
In Ireland, there were many secrets.

Family secrets -Illegitimacy, alcoholism,
mental illness, family feud
Kept within thick walls
neighbours could not penetrate.

After school, my friend whispered a terrible secret.
I vowed 'Cross my heart and hope to die'.
Such a burden that I feared
my talkative tongue would run with.
Some promises are hard to keep.

22
Present Giving

When I think of present giving, my mother's face floats into view. During the 1940s and 1950s in economically depressed Ireland, when many people scraped an existence or emigrated, my mother still managed to be a prolific present giver.

Our main income was from the shop and the very small rent from the Halloran's shop next door. This was years before supermarkets appeared to nearly put us out of business. There were always small amounts of cash about, hidden in different places in the house, and may have been designated for various things like 'First Communion' or 'Confirmation outfits'. If you told Mammy you loved *Girl Annual* or my brother hinted a need for more toy soldiers, she would do her best to get our desires for us, though it was not Christmas or a birthday. She often got into debt to give us presents.

It was not just the family that benefited from her generosity; she gave gifts to the poorest customers and often to the tinkers (now more often called travellers) such as fruit, which was a scarce luxury then, or clothes we had hardly worn and comics read once or twice. She was heartbroken when her great friend Hannah was hospitalised for years in a sanatorium with tuberculosis and separated from her young children. We would visit them regularly on Wednesday early closing day, laden with buns and sweets. Hannah's husband and her family did not forget this. They called Mammy their guardian angel.

Following her example, I too wanted to give presents. When I was young, I used to play with my friend Norah. Her family was not well off, and I wanted to give her a present. I had not given a present previously. Looking back, I cannot remember if it was for a birthday or not. I got permission to take a few coins from the metal box at the bottom of the chest of drawers. I spent ages down town choosing a book I thought Norah would like. She was so excited when I handed it to her.

Many years later Norah traced me through my old school in Ireland, who contacted my sister for my address. Norah was then a social worker and later became a Doctor of Psychology. and when she came with her son to stay with me in London, she told me, 'I will never forget that you gave me the first present I ever had.'

Norah Ashe with her beloved late mother.

23

Blackberries and Crubeens

Blackberries, lush and juicy
plucked from thorny bushes.
With purple stained hands
We fill our tin cans.

Exhausted, we trudge home
Mammy empties the cans
into the scale's scoop several times.
'You have earned two shillings.'

She tips the berries into a barrel
half full of crushed ones
in a mass of purple juice
destined for Co-Op jam.

Clutching our wealth
we avert our eyes from
the adjoining barrel
of crubeens in pickle
another of Mammy's earners.

Known as pigs' feet
customers clamoured for them
as they were cheap
but full of toes and bones.

Demand tailed off
we were left with dozens.
Fried, roasted, boiled, battered
I never ate one again.

24
Tralee Cinema 1940s-60s

Growing up in Tralee, the three cinemas were focal points in people's lives and especially my family. The *Picturedrome* in Upper Castle Street was nearby, the *Ashe Memorial Hall* was in Denny Street and the *Theatre Royal* was in Staughton's Row. There was no television then, so the cinemas were often packed, especially if there was a technicolour film as most films then were in black and white.

We had six free passes weekly, two for each cinema, as we displayed the film posters in our shop window. They showed only printed details of the weekly programme with no pictures. We could view scene shots from the films in the *Picturedrome* picture frames outside the doors. We went to the cinema frequently, sometimes we had to pay if we had used up the free passes.

The *Picturedrome* was our favourite being in our street. Many cinemagoers had little money and went into the cheap area called 'The Pit' which had uncomfortable seats and was too near the screen. It was said it smelt as well. We liked to go to the balcony, which gave a good view.

A film version of *Ulysses* was shown there once. I had no idea of the importance of the author of the book, James Joyce, and I am sure if the film was shown now, it would be filled to capacity. When I was about ten years old, I went to see it on my own as I could not get anyone to come with me and there was only one other person in the cinema – a man! It was so boring. All I can remember of it now is Milo O Shea's enormous bushy eyebrows.

The *Ashe Memorial Hall* doubled as a theatre as well. I recall having Irish dancing lessons on the stage from May Brassil. We spent more time playing hide and seek among the cinema seats than dancing.

The *Theatre Royal* did not live up to its grand name. The Coffey family who owned the *Picturedrome* ran it. When you entered the building, you passed through a massive dark, empty, space before entering the cinema, which had shabby seats and showed less popular films. When I got older and my siblings were not available to use the passes. I could often bring a friend with me.

Sunday evening was the big cinema night out, especially for couples. They liked to buy a quarter pound of Scots Clan or hard-boiled sweets to take with them. My parents were so busy in the shop that night to keep the queue down some sweets were weighed up in advance. We had a treat too as Mammy bought us comics such as *Girl, School Friend, Eagle, Dandy and Beano* as she and my father were too busy to tend to us during that busy period.

Sadly, when television came in, the cinemas were no longer the major entertainment in Tralee.

25
A New Beginning

Hated school
not like everyone,
Read a book a day
I wanted to do it my way.

Spelling, reading, writing
were my thing.
Algebra was not
as I usually got nought.

Relieved when age fifteen
My father said, 'No money
left to pay school fees
you can earn some pence.'

Jobs were scarce and got
by who you knew.
My Mother scoured the town
within days I had a position.

Hurley's Bookshop: newsagent, toys,
fancy goods, souvenirs, Maudella patterns,
records and tourist office,
It was enough to suffice.

Ann was newspapers and magazines
Miss O Brien records and stationary
Joan dealt with toys and window dressing
I with Irish Porcelain, cards and pens.

Variety, there certainly was.
When the boss found out I read,
she gave me books to critique
to entice customers to try them
and then buy.

26
The Corner Boys

They loitered about at Moyderwell Cross
and outside Healy's Diary
hands in pockets, fags in mouth,
usually on dole pay day.

No job or role in life
passing time scrutinising passers-by
whistling and name calling.

Longing for a whipped ice cream cone
I would advance slowly
eyes straight ahead.
Sudden barrage of muttering and cat calling
would make me tremor
Shouts of the dreaded 'Moko's daughter'
made me look down, tears prickling my sight.

In those vulnerable teenage years,
it seemed the deadliest insult
Now, in hindsight I wish I and my tormentors
had known it was only the name of a coffee.

27
Mammy the biggest influence in my life

There have been many people who have influenced my life, but the first and key person who comes to mind is my mother. I was the eldest of four so I was privy to secrets first. Looking back to when I was very young, I can recall how protective of us Mammy was, sometimes over the top. For instance, we had an early type of washing machine with a wringer which had to be turned manually. While using it I caught my fingers in it and Mammy got rid of it straight away so we never had another washing machine. We had a car and when I opened the door, nearly falling out, Mammy persuaded my father to get rid of it, so we never had another car either.

Now, reflecting on that, I do the opposite. I take things in my stride apart from one incident when I behaved like Mammy when the kids begged me to have fireworks. I got so scared handling them I said never again! Mammy was scared easily and I remember her going under the table when we had a thunder storm.

She had exceptional qualities that I admired and I have tried to take on board. Mammy was terrific with the public in our shop. She had time for everybody; the customers loved her and always stayed for a chat. We had no cash register for she could add up in her head and never make a mistake. Like her, I have always been interested in business and finances, perhaps because I worked in our shop and ran it when she was not well and. I went on to in retail for seven years before nurse training. I wonder what she would think about me now, retired and dabbling in antiques?

She was extremely generous and helped the poor so much. I have tried to be like that, but it would be difficult to be as good as she was. She was a terrific cook too and was always rushing in and out of the shop to stir the pots. My sister inherited her culinary skills, not me, but I definitely inherited her sense of adventure trying out new things.

She took us on so many outings and entertainments, including other children and relatives too. With all she did, housework was a low priority, when we were very young she had help, but could not afford it as we got older and our demands were greater. I think this influenced me in trying to do too much, but ending up doing everything.

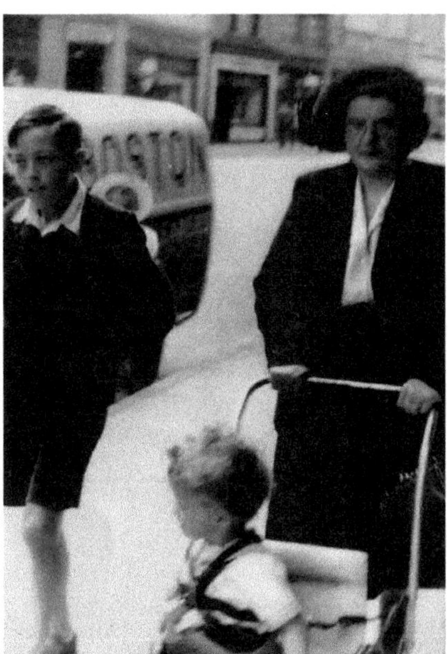

Mother (Mammy) about 1950.
Mammy & Victor in backyard about 1958.
Mammy with Victor in pushchair, cousin Ernie in Waterford.
Parents wedding day picture 1939.

28
My Mother Maisie Kelly and the *Rose of Tralee*

**Short memoir recorded by Green Curtain Theatre.
Recited by Marcella O Riordan on the Gerry Byrne show
IrishRadio.com and now on YouTube**

When I look back, the sun always shone when we were picking the fruit in the orchard of Cloghers House on the outskirts of Tralee. But that was because Mammy always made the summers fun for us.

We owned a shop on Upper Castle Street in the less fashionable end of town. Running a shop was hard work, profit was difficult to come by. Mammy, Maisie Kelly, was the centre of it all. There at the counter seven days a week, from six in the morning to eleven o'clock at night, never complaining. Mammy loved the chat and being an important part of people's lives. She was a brilliant listener, regarded as kindly, thought of with affection. Compliments richly deserved. Our customers were often poor, so she helped them in any way that she could. Gave people credit or extra goods for free, also our outgrown toys and clothes.

No one really knows who wrote the song *The Rose of Tralee.* For the people of Tralee, it was William Mulchinock, a poet from the family of wealthy merchants who once lived in Cloghers House. The song being inspired by Mary, a beautiful kitchen maid at their stately home. It is thought that the song's lyrics were adapted in part from another of Mulchinock's poems. There was a link with our shop and the House.

Fruit was expensive then and difficult to come by, but Cloghers House had a big orchard. Our cousin was friendly with the gardener. So, ever inspired Mammy struck a deal. We could sell their fruit in our shop - provided we picked it ourselves. And so, in the long summer holidays, we children would all head off with Mammy to spend hours picking gooseberries, apples and pears. And, out of sight, feast on their strawberries, which were far too expensive for us to even contemplate buying. Once picked, the fruit would be delivered in butter boxes and Mammy would haggle with the owner to secure a fair price before it was put out for sale.

The start of the Rose of Tralee competition in the 1950s combined with the annual Tralee Races changed the atmosphere in our usually quiet town. Streets became busier with visitors from all over Kerry. Pubs did a roaring trade. A wooden stage was erected in Denny Street for the entertainment. *The Harmonichords* who later became *The Bachelors* played for £5 a night to a tremendous reception. Shops like Mammy's were the 'go to place' for the chat and the buzz. At *Hurleys* large store, where I had started working, age fifteen, a 'mini tourist office' was created on the counter to 'cope with demand'. Tralee was alive. And Traleeans took the opportunity to come home for a visit. The poverty, high unemployment and migration which blighted us, was temporarily forgotten.

And we danced in the streets.

And we sang along, clapped with the bands and laughed even in the rain. We watched in wonder as the new 'Rose' was crowned at a dance. Mammy, ever the entrepreneur, made and sold sandwiches, served with red lemonade to the revellers. The whole town seemed happy.

My cousin Anne was a runner up one year and we were all thrilled. Today's 'Rose of Tralee' with all its glitz and glamour is very different from the festival I remember. No matter. It was what it was, and it suited us then. And it brought local people home, which was why it was started in the first place.

Sure, didn't the people of Tralee always know who the real roses were? People like Mammy the strong friendly Irish woman who made the place work.

29
Departures

I only feel I am home when
the train chugs into
Tralee Railway Station and
I step on to my beloved platform
at the end of the Kerry line.

From here many departures took place
hundreds of emigrants left for England.
My family too: My unsettled father
to London many times,
when we were young.

I waved as my sister travelled
to college in Dublin and my
brother too to Mallow and
later on John Bull's Isle.

My younger brother frequently
took the train seeking solace.

I occupied a window seat
for jobs in Killarney and Dublin.
Opportunities in Tralee were sparse then,
eventually left to nurse in Stoke-on-Trent.

My grandfather John Kelly
a domiciled Offaly man,
departed many times on his
Railway Guard duty.

One sad day
stepping on the line
between the buffers
of two trains,
crushed kidneys, the
death certificate stated.

The final departure.

30
Leaving Home

Leaving home and country was a fact of life in 1950s Ireland. In our town, it was a regular event. It was difficult to get work as the few jobs that were available were poorly paid, with little chance of advancement. It was who you knew that got you employment. Most young people left school at fifteen or even earlier, as secondary education had to be paid for and money was scarce.

If you could stay on and pass the Leaving Certificate and your parents could afford to send you to enrol in Mrs O Connor's Secretarial Course, you had a fair chance of getting a job in a solicitor's or a local merchant's office.

Some people went to the local technical college, but it was mostly for learning a trade and not considered prestigious at all and white-collar jobs were considered superior to working with your hands. University was in another world and not even discussed, in any case it had to be paid for and only children of professionals such as accountants, engineers or dentists went on to higher education. Ironically, they could be counted amongst the leavers too, as they all went to boarding school after they finished in primary school. When they returned home on holiday, they only mixed with their own compatriots and not with their former classmates.

What we used to call 'penny-ha'penny jobs' usually started at a pound a week. I had one of these in a local bookshop when I left school, aged fifteen. After a few years, pay might have reached a maximum of four pounds weekly, but even then, you could only afford to live at home.

For those who could not get a job, the only option was the migrant boat. For those who had relatives there, it might be America, but it was more likely to be London or Birmingham, perhaps Australia.

From our family shop we said farewell to many customers' adult children.

After a year away, the men would often swagger back dressed in a smart suit for their annual holiday. Now instead of muttering in an undertone for one Woodbine and a match, they would slam down a fiver on the scratched glass surface and cry out in an English accent for 'twenty Afton and a box of matches'. The female returnees might buy a quarter pound of Scots Clan, the quality chocolate toffees that were always a special treat. Before they emigrated, they would have probably bought twelve Aniseed Balls or a Cough-no-more for a penny. They seemed to have made it. We were all so envious.

Yet, while away, many had been secretly nostalgic for dillisk and the salted periwinkles we sold. On their return, we were often the first shop they visited.

Years later, when I was an emigrant myself, I soon realised that London and New York streets were not paved with gold and that the smart suit and twenty Afton were hard earned all year.

End Note

Welcome to the Potteries - originally appeared in my history of Irish nurses in Britain:

Ireland's Loss Britain's Gain - Irish Nurses in Britain Nightingale to Millennium

Published 2021

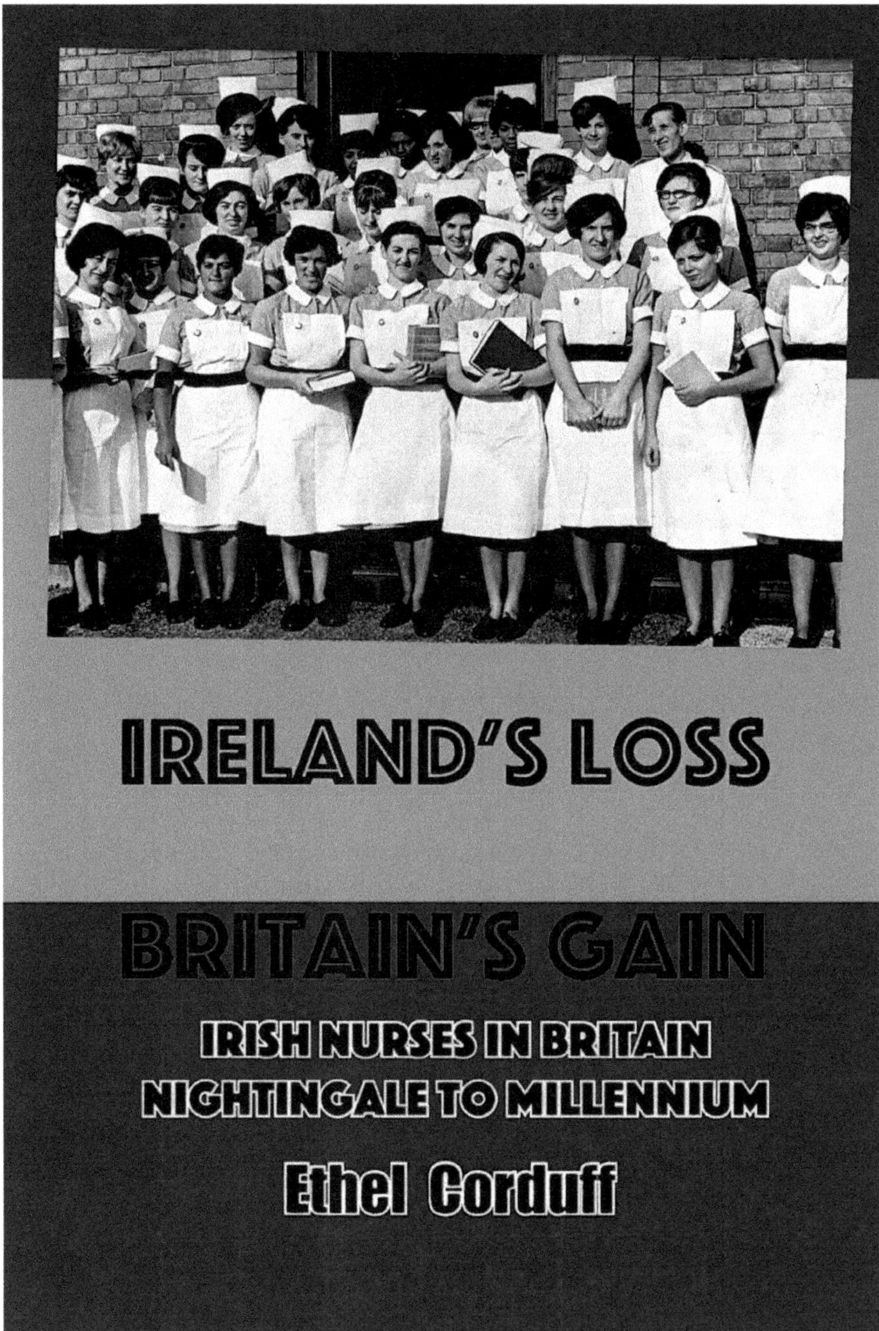
IRELAND'S LOSS
BRITAIN'S GAIN
IRISH NURSES IN BRITAIN
NIGHTINGALE TO MILLENNIUM
Ethel Corduff

Welcome to the Potteries

Goodbye green fields and open spaces
Rolling hills and local races
Clean air will be rare
When I get there

Liverpool station
Was a revelation
The journey via Crewe
Did not afford a happy view

Stoke on Trent, with hesitation
Was my distant destination
Dingy red brick and grey
Was this where I was to stay?

The pottery chimneys bellowed dark smoke
The first taste caused cough and choke
For coming years to inhale this air
Was more than I could bear

The people had a strange accent
Some vowels were clearly absent
They called us Duck
Perhaps with dreams of future pluck

One could walk for mile on mile
Past factory sites, not a single country style
Yet walking was better than the bus
Windows covered in industrial dust

The hospital like a fortress
Amongst the largest in the land
Health Service without much stress
For potters and miners at hand

Was this to be my lot?
I thought not
Compassionate nursing made me stay
To be trained myself, then on my way

The Photographs

What follows is a collection of the Author's family photographs.
Some were first shown in the text,
others are original or variations.
These monochrome images are a handful
of memories from an earlier age.

Captions where necessary for clarity.

Then and Now

Our shop at number 17 Upper Castle Street, is a Kebab shop and what was a jeweller's shop at number 16 and rented from us by the Halloran family is now a Laptop Clinic. Previously Frank's Fish and Chip Shop and Vincent's Coffee and Sandwich Bar were the occupants. Times change. (See next page for larger images.)

FRANK'S
Frank's 17

RAJAS
Raja's Kebab

LaptopPCclinic
Laptop & PC Clinic
SALES - REPAIRS - SERVICE
acer
SONY
VAIO
TOSHIBA
Computer
Repair
any brand, any problem
OPEN
LAPTOP REPAIRS

A studio Communion photo of Victor Walsh June 1957 (LEK037 ©Padraig & Joan Kennelly/Kennelly Archive).

Uncle Dennis Kelly, probably on his Communion Day.

Mammy

Aunt Hannah

Ethel at Kingdom County Fair about 1960.

Ethel and Margaret Dore at Kingdom County Fair about 1962.

My cousins Julie & Thady Tangney Ballydunlea with Cora O Connor and Marie Griffin about 1958.

Johnny and Mrs Dore with children Ann, Carmel and Assumpta.

Above: A fancy dress competition in Tralee 6th May 1954 (ESO05 ©Padraig and Joan Kennelly/Kennelly Archive).
Below: Cowboy and girl holding cottage. A fancy dress competition in Tralee 6th May 1954 (ESO14 © Padraig & Joan Kennelly/Kennelly Archive).

A fancy dress competition in Tralee 6th May 1954. (EW015 ©Padraig and Joan Kennelly/Kennelly Archive.)

Ethel in Irish dancing costume, sister Gloria on raffle prize tricycle.

Town Park bench Switzer brothers, Margaret Mason, Eddie, Ethel, Glória, Bernard and Vourneen Flaherty 1950s.
Below: Ethel's Infants Class about 1946, Ethel wearing gymslip seated front row second from right.

Mammy with Victor in pushchair with cousin Ernie in Waterfood.
Right: Ethel aged about three.
The Mall Tralee about 1949 Mammy, Eddie in pushchair, Gloria, Mrs Prendeville and daughter.

Ethel about 1952, aged 10, in the Mall, Tralee.

Mammy outside Revington's 1950s – we call this picture 'Mammy coming out of jail'.

Mammy with pram in the 1950s.

Mammy, with Gloria in a pushchair about 1950.

Above: Gloria, Eddie, Ina Murray about 1950.
Left: Ethel and Eddie about 1950.

Ethel First Communion pictures 1949.

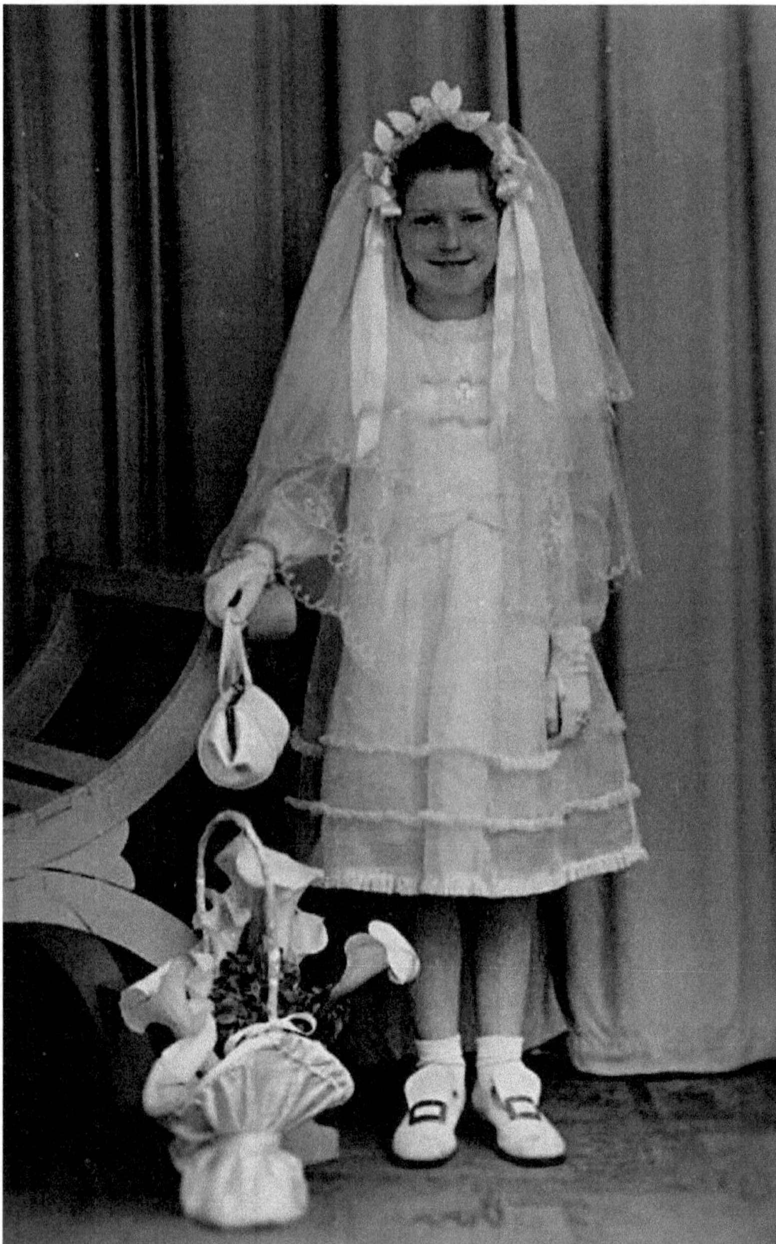

Ethel First Communion pictures 1949.

Above: Fancy dress entrants at the Back Yard Bazaar.
Below: Jill Mason and Victor with dillisk.

Eileen Dore, Cora O Connor, Ethel outside Presentation School about 1957.
Ethel & Marie Murray about 1950.
Group of school friends 1957.

School friends 1957.

Ethel's confirmation.

Angel holy water fonts, St John's Church,

Victor with dog in backyard 1958.
Victor and Ethel 1958.
Ethel and Cora O Connor (Ethel with new bike).

Gloria dancing with Victor about 1956.

Ethel outside McCowens 1952.

Ethel & friend Nellie Lynch.

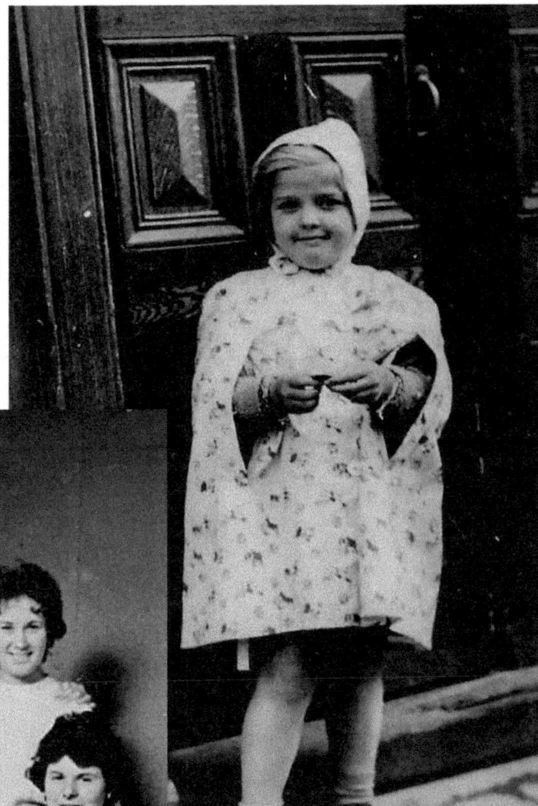

Gloria outside McCowens 1952.

Work colleagues from Hurleys friend leaving for America 1960s.

Ethel at 18.

Dad in his favourite chair, probably reading the *Irish Times*.

Ethel and Mammy in our front room.

Ethel outside Presentation Convent School 1990s.

Sin é